First published in North America in 2014 by Boxer Books Limited.
First published in Great Britain in 2011 by PatrickGeorge.
www.boxerbooks.com

Text and illustrations copyright © 2011 PatrickGeorge.

The right of Patrick George to be identified as the author and
illustrator of this work has been asserted by him in accordance
with the Copyright, Designs and Patents Act, 1988.

The illustrations were prepared digitally by PatrickGeorge.
The text is set in ITC Avant Garde Gothic.

ISBN 978-1-907967-94-8

1 3 5 7 9 10 8 6 4 2

Printed in China

MAGIC NUMBERS

BOXER BOOKS

ten

nine

eight

7

seven

6

six

5

five

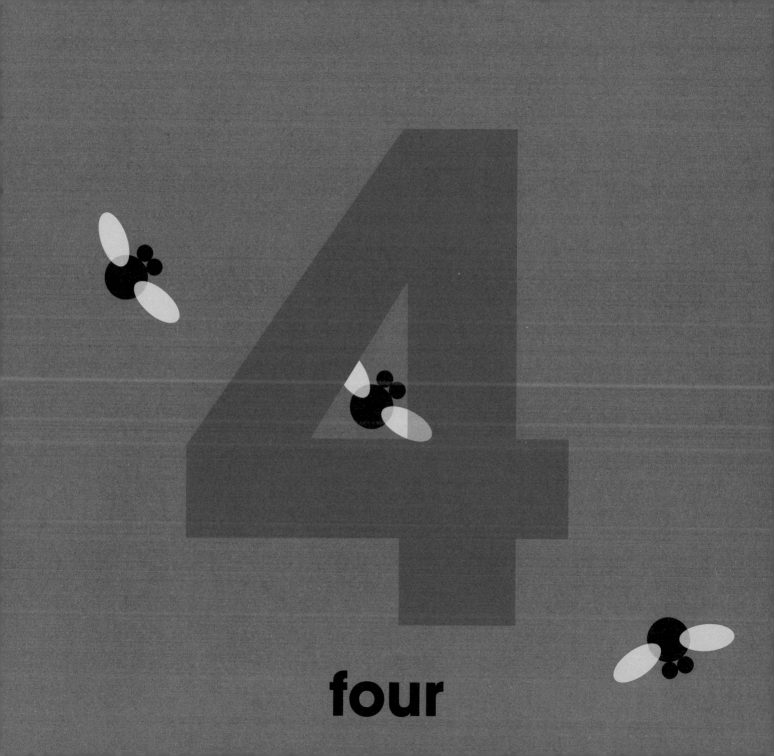

four

3

three

two

two

1

one

zero